The Physiological Effects of Human and Companion Animal Interactions

Written by

Karen Whiteley FdSc, BSc (Hons)

Other books by Karen Whiteley

This paperback edition published in 2013

ISBN-13: 978 1490461014

Contents

1.0 Introduction

As of 2008 there were 27 million pets in the UK with dogs (7.3 million) and cats (7.2 million) being the animal of choice for many pet owners. Since 1980 this figure has climbed from 5.6 million and 4.9 million respectively and over the centuries human attitudes and their perception of animals has changed dramatically.

The domestication of wolves (*Canis lupus*) occurred approximately 500,000 years ago. Originally wolves and humans were competitors for prey but by taming the wolf, man was able to use their ability to track and detect prey. However, the bond between the two species strengthened and evidence from archaeological remains of a joint burial 12,000 years ago shows a clear association between the two species. Similarly, research by Vigne *et al.* (2004) found evidence of a joint burial of a cat and human 8,300 years ago which too suggests a bond between the two.

Historically animals were required to work for their keep but this is not generally the case for Western companion animals. Nevertheless, there is evidence to suggest that humans do benefit from becoming pet owners and this report will evaluate the physiological effects of human and companion animal interactions.

2.0 Why Keep Companion Animals?

A survey carried out by the Pet Food Manufacturers' Association shows that 60% of single people in the UK obtain a pet for companionship with 39% of people stating that they had replaced a partner with a pet. The survey also found that in London, 39% of pet owners obtained the pet for companionship despite the City being home to 7.5 million people.

There are several theories of why the human and animal relationship has grown within Western societies. Firstly, the increasing demand for the companionship of animals may result from people becoming isolated from one another, for example, technology is reducing human interaction. Secondly, increasing media coverage of crime, war and terrorism has taught humans to be vigilant and wary of one another, therefore people are reluctant to trust others or form relationships. Thirdly, neighbourhoods were historically places where families shared history and culture but with the increasing movement of populations, people may no longer know others outside of work and in some cases, only superficial relationships with co-workers exist. As a consequence, companion animals are the only family that some people have. Still, there is research to suggest that humans obtain both physiological as well as psychological benefits from owning pets, although most of the research is conducted in Western societies.

In a study carried out by Serpell (1991), as well as the health benefits from physically walking a dog, dog owners also reported benefits of reduced stress and depression including reduced fear of crime and improved self-esteem. Furthermore, both dog and cat owners expressed fewer emotional concerns, non-judgemental companionship, physical contact with another living species and factors that contribute towards wellbeing such as fun and laughter which in turn reduces depression and anxiety.

Social contact between pets and people is recognised as being beneficial as it alleviates feelings of loneliness and social isolation. This is particularly important for people at risk of social isolation such as the elderly, people with physical disabilities or people who lack the opportunity to interact socially. Quality of life may also be improved through shared pleasure in recreation and relaxation. Pets may enhance social interaction with other humans which provides an indirect benefit on wellbeing. The relationship with pets also seems to be beneficial during stressful experiences such as the early stages of bereavement and after cancer treatment.

3.0 Physiological Effects of Pet Ownership

3.1 *Long Term Effects*

Friedmann (1995) states '*social, psychological and physiological factors are now widely recognised as factors influencing the development and progression of many chronic or stress related diseases*'. Pets may aid owners by decreasing the impact of the stress, therefore decreasing anxiety and blood pressure or help remove the built up stress hormones from the owners' body by encouraging exercise.

Four epidemiological studies have shown the influence pets can have on the cardiovascular health of their owners. An example from a study carried out by Friedmann *et al.* (1980) indicates that pet owners were more likely to survive one year after discharge from coronary care compared to non-pet owners. However, the type of pet may provide different benefits (figure 1), for example, dog owners were approximately 8.6 times more likely to survive one year after discharge compared to those that did not own dogs (p<0.002). Social support was also a significant indicator of survival (p<0.05). After dog owners were omitted from the study due to the additional health benefits (e.g. physical exercise) the percentage of pet owners alive one year after discharge from hospital was still higher.

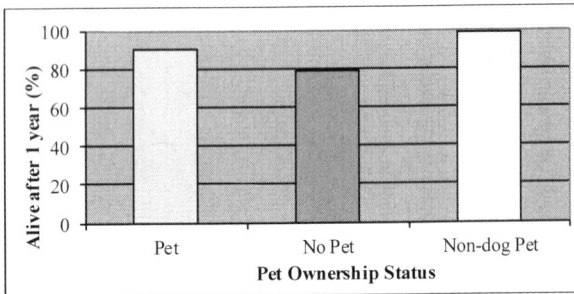

Figure 1. Comparison of 1 year survival rates after admission to a coronary care unit between pet owners, non-owners and owners of a 'non-dog' pet (adapted from: Friedmann, 1995)

In contrast, cat owners were more likely to die than non-pet owners ($p<0.03$), as cat owners were associated with lower social support ($P<0.01$). Additional health benefits from being a dog owner include increased physical exercise due to walking the dog, compared to cat owners who were more likely to relax with their pet. Additionally, more time is devoted to a dog, as cats are considered more independent; therefore, dog owners may lead a less stressful lifestyle.

Additional benefits from owning a pet include:

- Lower use of general practitioner services.

- Reduced risk of asthma and allergic rhinitis in children exposed to pet allergens during the first year of life.

- Reduced risk of cardiovascular disease.

- Lower blood pressure responses to psychological stress.

- Exposure to harmful bacteria can build immunity.

- Pet owners appear to be more resilient to stressful events, resulting in fewer heath problems.

- Increased physical activity due to walking or playing with the pet.

- Promote responsible living.

- Provide social support.

- Promote factors that contribute to well being e.g. encourage laughter and provide owners with fun and entertainment.

However, negative aspects of pet ownership should also be taken into consideration:

- Stress caused when trying to manage an unruly animal.

- Owners taking better care of their pet than themselves which may result in health implications.

- Injury caused by the animal e.g. minor injuries such as scratches and major injuries such as bites or kicks.

- Financial stress e.g. the cost of pet food, veterinary bills, damage to furniture.

- Allergic reactions to animals.

- Hygiene problems e.g. not grooming / cleaning the animals or environment / equipment correctly e.g. litter tray.

- Zoonotic diseases e.g. toxoplasmosis.

- Previous experiences with specific animals.

- Time needed to care for the animal.

A further questionnaire based study carried out by Serpell (1991) monitored new pet owners over a period of ten months to determine whether pet ownership is beneficial to human health. Health problems that were included in the questionnaire are as follows:

Headaches, nerves, palpitations, hay fever, colds and flu, difficulty concentrating, difficulty sleeping, general tiredness, worrying, constipation, breathlessness, indigestion or other stomach problems, eye problems, painful joints, kidney or bladder problems, back problems, ear problems, sinus or catarrh problems, persistent cough, faint or dizziness, feet problems.

The results from the study found that new pet owners experienced significantly less minor health problems one month after adopting the pet. However, dog owners maintained this decrease over the ten month study whereas cat owners did not. This outcome may result from dog owners undertaking more physical activity and again like the study carried out by Friedmann *et al.* (1980) dog owners may lead a less stressful lifestyle and have available time to walk and care for their animal. Cat owners generally choose a cat as a pet because they lead a faster paced lifestyle and require an animal which is more independent.

3.2 Short Term Effects

Unlike the long term effects of animal ownership, short term effects are measured in minutes rather than months or years. Short term studies have been carried out in order to prove that observing animals, looking at pictures of animals, being in the presence of animals and interacting with animals can reduce physiological responses to stressors.

A short term study carried out by Lockwood (1983) looked into the effects of humans looking at pictures of animals. The first study showed a scene with only human(s) situated in a natural setting. The second study showed identical pictures but this time with animal(s) present. Results showed that the pictures with animals present made the people in the pictures appear significantly more friendly, happier and less threatening.

Many of the studies focussing on the short term impact that animals have on human physiology are mainly focussed on the impact that dogs have on human health due to this pets' popularity (convenience) and the fact that they are easier to handle. However, research conducted by Eddy (1996) demonstrated the cardiovascular effects of observing animals using a pet snake. The blood pressure and heart rate of a twenty-six year old male snake owner was monitored and it was found that during the six minute study both heart rate and blood pressure lowered while the pet owner was observing the snake. Although, when the same pet owner, in a later study, was able to touch the snake the subject's blood pressure during the six minute case study lowered further.

Baun *et al.* (1984) studied the effects on an owner petting an unfamiliar animal compared to the owner's own pet. It was found that blood pressure significantly decreased when the participant petted their own dog but it did not fall significantly when they petted an unfamiliar animal. Although, when the owner initially interacted and greeted the pet blood pressure was higher. Freidmann (2000) suggests that if this is taken into account the variance in responses to the participants own compared to other dogs may not be significant.

Still, these studies do not take into consideration other life events, for example, other types of social support or other aspects of psychological and physical health, therefore these other factors should be addressed before firm conclusions are made of whether pet ownership benefits human health. Also, they do not take into account previous experience with specific species of animals. Neither do they explore cultural attitudes towards animals, for example, in parts of the Far East dogs and cats are used for food but in contrast the cow is sacred in India and it

is forbidden to kill or consume it.

4.0 Conclusion

There is evidence to suggest that owning pets can be beneficial on human health. In particular, epidemiological studies have shown the influence that pets can have on the cardiovascular health of their owners. Obtaining a pet is associated with fewer health complaints, better one year survival of patients after myocardial infarctions, lower blood pressure and provide social support to name but a few. Short term studies have also found that petting and looking at animals also reduces blood pressure. This effect is seen with humans and unfamiliar animals but is most prominent when there is a bond between the pet and owner.

However, owning a dog is thought to be more beneficial than owning a cat which may result from dog owners having a more active lifestyle.

References

Anderson, P.E. (2008) *The Powerful Bond between Pets and People*. United States of America: Praeger Publishers

Baun, M.M., Bergstrom, N., Langston, N.F. and Thoma, L. (1984) 'Physiological effects of human/companion animal bondig' *Nursing Research* **33** pp. 126-129. Cited in: Podberscek, A.L., Paul, E.S., and Serpell, J.A.(2000) *Companion Animals and Us: exploring the relationships between people and pets*. Cambridge: Cambridge University Press

Clutton-Brock, J. (1995) Origins of the dog: domestication and early history. In: Serpell, J. (ed.) *The Domestic Dog; its evolution, behaviour and interactions with people*. Cambridge: Cambridge University Press

Cusack, O. (1988) *Pets and Mental Health*. New York: The Haworth Press

Eddy, T.J. (1996) 'Reductions in Cardiac Activity in Response to a Pet Snake' *Journal of Nervous and Mental Disease* **184** pp. 573-575. Cited in: In: Podberscek, A.L., Paul, E.S., and Serpell, J.A.(2000) *Companion Animals and Us: exploring the relationships between people and pets*. Cambridge: Cambridge University Press

Friedmann, E. (1995) 'The Role of Pets in Enhancing Human Well-being: Physiological Effects'. In: Robinson, I. (ed.) (1995) *The Waltham Book of Human-Animal Interaction: Benefits and responsibilities of pet ownership.* United Kingdom: Elsevier Science Limited

Friedmann, E., Katcher, A.H., Lynch, J.J. and Thomas, S.A. (1980) 'Animals companions and one year survival of patients after discharge from a coronary care unit' *Public Health Reports* **95** pp. 307-312. Cited in: Robinson, I. (ed.) (1995) *The Waltham Book of Human-Animal Interaction: Benefits and responsibilities of pet ownership.* United Kingdom: Elsevier Science Limited

Friedmann, E., Thomas, S.A., Eddy, T.J. (2000) *Companion Animals and Human Health; physical and cardiovascular influences.* In: Podberscek, A.L., Paul, E.S., and Serpell, J.A.(2000) *Companion Animals and Us: exploring the relationships between people and pets.* Cambridge: Cambridge University Press

Koler-Matznick, J. (2002) 'The Origin of the Dog Revisited' *Anthrozoos* **15**(2) pp. 98-118

Lockwood, R. (1983) 'The influence of animals on social perception'. Cited in: Podberscek, A.L., Paul, E.S., and Serpell, J.A.(2000) *Companion Animals and Us: exploring the relationships between people and pets.* Cambridge: Cambridge University Press

McNicholas, J., Gilbey, A., Rennie, A, Ahmedzai, S., Dono, J.A. amd Ormerod (2005) 'Pet Ownership and Human Health: a brief review of evidence and issues' *British Medical Journal* **331** pp.1252-1254

Parslow, R.A. and Jorm, A.F. (2003) 'Pet ownership and risk factors for cardiovascular disease: another look' *Medical Journal of Australia* **179** pp. 466-468

PFMA [Pet Food Manufacturers' Association] (2008) *Pet Population Figures* [online] Available at <http://www.pfma.org.uk/overall/pet-population-figures-2.htm> [Accessed 05 February 2009]

Robinson, I. (ed.) (1995) *The Waltham Book of Human-Animal Interaction: Benefits and responsibilities of pet ownership*. United Kingdom: Elsevier Science Limited

Serpell, J.A. (2003) 'Anthropomorphism and Anthropomorphic Selection – Beyond the "Cute Response"' *Society and Animals* **11**(1) pp. 83-100 [online] Available at <http://www.animalsandsociety.org/assets/library/495_s1 117.pdf> Accessed 03 February 2009

Serpell, J.A. (1991) 'Beneficial effects of pet ownership on some aspects of human health' *Journal of the Royal Society of Medicine* **84** pp. 717-720. Cited in: Robinson, I. (ed.) (1995) *The Waltham Book of Human-Animal Interaction: Benefits and responsibilities of pet ownership*. United Kingdom: Elsevier Science Limited

Vigne, J.D., Guilaine, J., Debue, K., Haye, L. and Gerard, P. (2004) 'Early taming of the cat in Cyprus' *Science* **304** pp. 259

<u>Notes</u>

Notes

12630147R00022

Printed in Great Britain
by Amazon.co.uk, Ltd.,
Marston Gate.